BETTER BASKETBALL

A GUIDE FOR THE SERIOUS COACH AND PLAYER

Joe Williams

Sterling Publishing Co., Inc.   New York
Distributed in the U.K. by Blandford Press

A SPORTS PUBLICATION BY THE ATHLETIC INSTITUTE

Demonstrators
Florida State University
Purdue University

Distributed by
Sterling Publishing Co., Inc.
2 Park Avenue, New York, New York 10016

Copyright © 1983 The Athletic Institute

Distributed in Australia by Oak Tree Press Co., Ltd.
P.O. Box K514 Haymarket, Sydney 2000, N.S.W.
Distributed in the United Kingdom by Blandford Press
Link House, West Street, Poole, Dorset BH15 1LL, England
Distributed in Canada by Oak Tree Press Ltd.
c/o Canadian Manda Group, P.O. Box 920, Station U
Toronto, Ontario, Canada M8Z 5P9

Library of Congress Catalog Card Number 83-70282
ISBN 0-8069-7788-4

A WORD FROM THE PUBLISHER

THIS SPORTS PUBLICATION, is but one item in a comprehensive list of sports instructional aids, such as video cassettes, 16mm films, 8mm silent loops and filmstrips which are made available by The Athletic Institute. This book is part of a master plan which seeks to make the benefits of athletics, physical education and recreation available to everyone.

The Athletic Institute is a not-for-profit organization devoted to the advancement of athletics, physical education and recreation. The Institute believes that participation in athletics and recreation has benefits of inestimable value to the individual and to the community.

The nature and scope of the many Institute programs are determined by a Professional Advisory Committee, whose members are noted for their outstanding knowledge, experience and ability in the fields of athletics, physical education and recreation.

The Institute believes that through this book the reader will become a better performer, skilled in the fundamentals of this fine event. Knowledge and the practice necessary to mold knowledge into playing ability are the keys to real enjoyment in playing any game or sport.

Howard J. Bruns
President and Chief Executive Officer
The Athletic Institute

D. E. Bushore
Executive Director
The Athletic Institute

Philosophy

If I could use only one word to describe my basketball coaching philosophy, it would be unselfishness.

We teach our players to constantly be watching for the scoring play when they have the ball. While always looking for an open man, a player may continue toward the basket and try to score when no opponent picks him up.

A one-on-one player who does not pass the ball is a detriment to his coach and to his teammates. In fact, no one will want him on his team. But if you have an outstanding player and you can work on his moves and improve his self-image as a shooter, you will have an even better player. He sees that by improving his all-around skills he is becoming a better basketball player. The bond between coach and player will become stronger as he gains from the experience and his talents become more useful in your offense.

The best one-on-one players are usually the best passers and they will lead your team in assists.

As many other coaches, I also stress hard work and movement without the basketball. A player may not realize that in a typical game, he may have his hands on the ball only one-tenth of the time. That's just four minutes in a college game (40 minutes) and just over three minutes in a high school game (32 minutes).

We ask our players to think about what they are doing to help us win the game for the 36 minutes when they don't have the ball. It is as important to be a good passer, a good defensive player, to rebound well and to keep your man off the boards, as it is to be a good shooter.

Half of the game is spent on defense and each player may handle the ball only about one-fifth of the offensive time. What he does without the ball is very important in contributing to a victory. Many times a ball is lost to the opposing team because the receiver did not get open to take a pass. He has to learn to move without the ball to be able to get open to receive the ball.

It is a good idea in pick-up games for players to work on different parts of their games, such as defense, rebounding and passing, instead of wasting time out on the floor by just standing around without the ball. This is an excellent way to develop better habits which can be used during a game to help your team win.

Again, let me emphasize — we always stress unselfishness.

Joe Williams
Head Coach
Florida State University

In his first 18 years as a college head coach — at Jacksonville (Fla.) University, Furman University in Greenville, S.C., and Florida State University in Tallahassee — Williams' overall record was 303 wins and 195 losses, a 61 percent winning edge. Williams played at Oklahoma City University, got his bachelor's degree at Southern Methodist University in 1957 and his master's degree from the University of Florida in 1968.

Table of Contents

Rules Simplified

Basic Stances

Basic Offensive Stance

The *basic offensive stance,* sometimes referred to as
the **ready position,** gives a player three avenues of attack: 1) to drive on a defender (dribble), 2) to shoot
over a defender, 3) to pass to a teammate.

This position affords proper body balance with feet
a shoulder's-width apart and one foot slightly ahead
of the other. Head is up. shoulders are square to the
basket and knees are slightly flexed. Ball is held firmly
from chest to waist level.

1. BASIC OFFENSIVE STANCE
   Feet Are Shoulder's Width Apart.
   One Foot Slightly Ahead of the
       Other.
   Head Up.
   Shoulders and Body Square to Hoop
   Ball Held Firmly at Chest Level.

2. FROM BASIC OFFENSIVE STANCE, PLAYER MAY
   REACT QUICKLY FOR DRIVE TO BASKET, SHOOT
   IF OPEN OR PASS TO TEAMMATE.

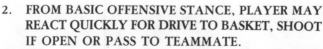

Basic Defensive Stance

Like the offensive ready position, the *basic defensive stance* requires proper body position and weight distribution to the changing defensive situation.

A defender must be ready to counter the three basic options available to the offensive player — the drive, shot or pass. Good defense involves anticipation of the next movement by the offensive player and quick reactions to move and control these movements effectively.

As a defensive player, position yourself just beyond a normal arm's reach

1. **DEFENSIVE READY POSITION**
   Body Balanced with Weight Equally Distributed on Both Feet.
   Feet are Shoulder's-Width Apart with One Foot Slightly Ahead of the Other.
   Knees Are Flexed.
   Arms Are Relatively Close to Body.
   Head Is Up with Eyes Focused Ahead.

from the opponent with the ball, then make the necessary adjustments to the opponent's moves. From this point it is a matter of anticipating what the defender is going to do and reacting accordingly.

To overplay an opponent effectively, take one half-step to the side which you wish to defend. Proper defensive movement employs a sliding action of the feet. Take your first step in the direction in which the opponent starts his move. Your second step is a sliding step to bring you into a control position. This sequence is then repeated as required.

When guarding a man without the ball, adjust your position so you see both your opponent and the ball on the court. Any movement of the offensive player must be countered. Any movement of the ball most likely will require an adjustment on your part. Preventing ''your man'' from getting the ball at all is your best defense.

2. **OVERPLAY OPPONENT ONE HALF-STEP TO THE SIDE YOU WISH TO DEFEND.**

3. USE STEP, SLIDING-STEP ACTION TO ACHIEVE CONTROL POSITION.
4. CLOSE TO POSITION IN DRIBBLER'S PATH.

5. WHEN DEFENDING AGAINST SHOOTER, RAISE CLOSEST HAND AND MOVE TO TIGHTER POSITION. LIKEWISE, WHEN DEFENDING AGAINST PASS, REACT WITH HAND CLOSEST TO SOURCE OF PASS.

Dribble

Basic Dribble Position

A **ready position** is fundamental to executing both the *Control* and *Speed Dribbles*. In this position, the head is up, knees are flexed, eyes focus down floor, and the body is in a semi-crouched position. The degree of body crouch varies according to the speed of the dribble and the conditions under which the dribbler performs.

The finger and thumb tips contact the ball. The hand is on top of the ball toward the back half of the top surface.

BASIC DRIBBLE POSITION
   Head Up; Eyes Focus Ahead.
   Knees Flexed; Body in Semi-
      Crouched Position.
   Ball Contacted with Fingers
      and Thumb Tips.
   Free Arm is Out for Balance
      and Ball Protection.

Control Dribble

Begin by projecting the ball slightly forward using fingertip control. Fingertip control is executed by flexing of the wrist and fingers. The lower arm from the elbow to fingertips moves in a pumping action to project, receive and then project the ball again.

Dribble the ball knee- to waist-high to gain better control and reduce the opponent's chance of stealing it. Again, protect the ball with the arm and leg nearest your opponent.

9

1. ASSUME READY POSITION.
2. PROJECT BALL SLIGHTLY FORWARD USING FINGERTIP CONTROL AND LOWER ARM PUMP-ING ACTION.
3. DRIBBLE KNEE TO WAIST HIGH.
4. PROTECT BALL WITH ARM AND LEG.

Speed Dribble

Certain adjustments need to be made for executing a Speed Dribble effectively.

As the ball is dribbled, lean your body more forward and into the dribble. Control the ball from waist to chest level.

Keep your shoulders square to the direction of travel while protecting ball with your arm and leg.

1. **FROM BASIC DRIBBLE READY POSITION, LEAN FORWARD AND INTO DRIBBLE.**
2. **CONTROL BALL FROM WAIST- TO CHEST-HIGH.**

3. **KEEP SHOULDERS SQUARE TO DIRECTION OF TRAVEL.**
4. **PROTECT BALL WITH ARM AND LEG.**

11

Changing Directions

Reverse Pivot Change Techniques

From a Control Dribble, begin the *Reverse Pivot Change* by stopping temporarily on the foot opposite the dribbling hand. Legs are flexed at the knees with body weight slightly forward on the extended foot.

Pivot on balls of both feet while shifting weight to the extended foot. In making the pivot, transfer ball to the opposite hand. Now begin dribble, close to the floor as well as to the body.

In reversing the ball from side to side, protect the ball with the arm and leg nearest your opponent.

1. BEGIN CHANGE FROM CONTROL DRIBBLE.
2. STOP ON FOOT OPPOSITE DRIBBLING HAND.
3. PIVOT ON FRONT FOOT.
4. TRANSFER BALL TO OPPOSITE HAND.
5. COMPLETE PIVOT ON OPPOSITE FOOT.
6. PROTECT BALL WITH ARM AND LEG.

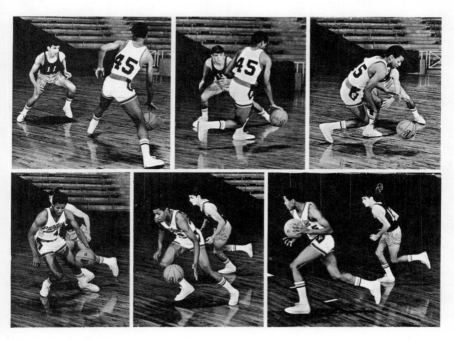

Crossover Change Techniques

After learning the Control Dribble, develop methods of changing direction while dribbling. Execute the *Crossover Change* by bouncing the ball to the opposite hand. The shoulders are square to the direction of travel. Drive off the trailing leg and protect the ball with the free hand, arm and leg nearest opponent.

1. BEGIN CHANGE FROM CONTROL DRIBBLE.
2. BOUNCE BALL SHARPLY TO OPPOSITE HAND.
3. SQUARE SHOULDERS TO DIRECTION OF TRAVEL.
4. EXCHANGE MUST BE MADE QUICKLY SINCE BALL IS EXPOSED TO OPPONENT FOR BRIEF INSTANT.
5. DRIVE OFF TRAILING LEG.
6. PROTECT BALL WITH ARM AND LEG.

Side View (Crossover Change Techniques)

Passing

Chest Pass Techniques

The *Chest Pass* is made from a **ready position**, i.e., flexed knees, facing target, head up and eyes on intended receiver.

Ball is held at chest level with the hands placed above and slightly behind the center of the ball. Elbows are bent.

Grip the ball with the fingers and thumbs, keeping the palms of the hands off the ball.

Step to target and simultaneously execute a quick downward then upward motion with the hands to cock the wrists.

Uncock the wrists by pronating the wrists inward with the thumbs down. Keep the trajectory of the ball on a level plane.

1. **READY POSITION**
    Flex Knees.
    Face Target.
    Head Up.
    Eyes on Receiver.
    Ball at Chest Level.
    Bend Elbow.
    Grip with Fingertips.

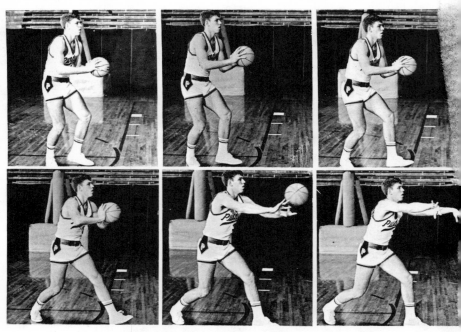

2. STEP TO TARGET AND RELEASE BALL.
3. PRONATE WRISTS INWARD WITH THUMBS
   DOWN UPON RELEASE.

Two-Hand Bounce Pass

The *Two-Handed Bounce Pass* is merely a variation of the Chest Pass in that the ball is projected to the floor so that a teammate receives it after it has bounced once.

Otherwise all Chest Pass techniques apply.

1. APPLY ALL CHEST PASS TECHNIQUES TO PROJECT BALL ON ONE BOUNCE TO TEAMMATE.
2. AVOID "TELEGRAPHING" PASS.

23

One-Hand Flip Pass

This pass is sometimes referred to as a *Hook Pass* because such a pass is very often effective in getting the ball around a closely guarding defender.

Like the Chest Pass, the *One-Handed Flip Pass* may be delivered on a level trajectory or made to bounce once to a teammate. Often the bounce pass is the safer pass to make.

From the **ready position,** step out to the side of the defender where you intend to release the pass. With eyes on the receiver, grip the ball firmly in both hands until the point of release. Project the ball with the outside hand and pronate the wrist over the top of the ball to release the ball with a "flipping action."

1. FROM READY POSITION WITH EYES ON RECEIVER, STEP TO SIDE OF INTENDED PASS.
2. KEEP BOTH HANDS ON BALL UNTIL POINT OF RELEASE.
3. PRONATE WRIST OF OUTSIDE HAND OVER TOP OF BALL TO MAKE RELEASE WITH "FLIPPING ACTION."
4. DELIVER BALL ON LEVEL TRAJECTORY OR BOUNCE TO TEAMMATE.

One-Hand Flip Pass with Crossover Step

Some players prefer to execute a Hook Pass with a crossover step. Such a maneuver may be slightly more difficult to execute; however, it does provide greater protection in that the side of the body is turned to a tightly guarding defender. The shoulder, arm and leg are between the ball and defender, affording increased protection.

The mechanics of delivery are the same as for the One-Hand Flip Pass described before.

1. TURN SIDE OF BODY TO DEFENDER BY STEPPING TO SIDE OF INTENDED PASS WITH CROSSOVER STEP.
2. SHOULDER, ARM AND LEG AFFORD PROTECTION BETWEEN DEFENDER AND BALL
3. RELEASE BALL ON LEVEL TRAJECTORY OR BOUNCE TO TEAMMATE.

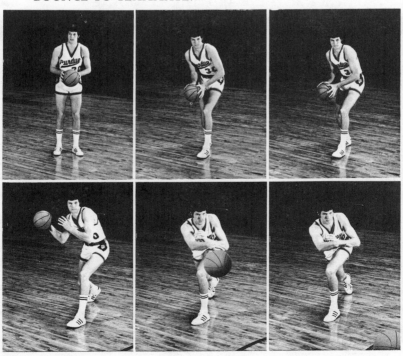

Overhead Pass Techniques

The *Overhead Pass* is also executed from a **ready position** which includes facing the target, head up, eyes on receiver, and gripping the ball with fingertips. Often, such a pass is made after a pivot to achieve a ready position.

From the position extend the arms upward, with the ball above and slightly in front of the head. Upon delivery step to target, simultaneously rotating, the fingers back and down to cock the wrists.

Uncock the wrists by pronating the wrist inward with thumbs down. The pass should be received approximately chest-high.

1. READY POSITION: FACE TARGET WITH HEAD UP AND EYES ON RECEIVER. GRIP BALL WITH FINGERTIPS.
2. EXTEND ARMS UPWARD WITH BALL OVERHEAD. STEP TO TARGET.
3. PRONATE WRISTS INWARD, THUMBS DOWN.

Baseball Pass Techniques

Such a pass is executed from the basic offensive stance very often after the passer has pivoted to face the receiver. A *Baseball Pass* may be thrown farther than any other pass; however, control and accuracy may be sacrificed if the pass is not made properly and prudently.

To throw this pass, draw the ball over your throwing shoulder and behind your ear. Extend your free arm toward the receiver while stepping out with the forward foot.

The ball is thrust forward while your weight is transferred from the back foot to the foward foot. Release the ball at full-arm extension as the

leg on the throwing side comes forward to achieve a balanced follow-through. Note that the release is executed through fingertip control and wrist snap.

The free hand is proximate to the point of release should you decide to control the ball rather than throw the pass.

1. FROM READY POSITION, DRAW BALL OVER THROWING SHOULDER AND BEHIND EAR.
2. EXTEND FREE ARM TOWARD RECEIVER AND STEP FORWARD
3. TRANSFER WEIGHT FROM BACK FOOT TO FORWARD FOOT AND RELEASE BALL AT FULL-ARM EXTENSION.
4. BRING BACK LEG FORWARD, INTO BALANCED FOLLOW-THROUGH POSITION.
5. FINGERTIP CONTROL AND WRIST SNAP ARE ESSENTIAL ELEMENTS FOR EFFECTIVE PASS.
6. FREE HAND PROXIMATE TO BALL SHOULD YOU DECIDE NOT TO CONTINUE WITH THROW.

Shooting

The Basic Shot

The basic, starting position for shooting is similar to catching the ball in the "basic offensive stance" described earlier.

Regardless of the type of shot which will be taken, ball position is the same. The upper arm is parallel to the floor and the forearm is bent at a 90 degree angle. The wrist is cocked with the shooting hand slightly under and behind the ball. In this position, the shoulder, elbow, hand and ball should be lined up toward the target. It is especially important that while keeping these parts of the arm in a lever position before taking a shot you do not let the elbow get too far away, laterally, from the side of the body. A flying elbow changes the angle of the shot and this can affect aim and ball control.

The target is the middle of the basket, halfway between the front and back of the rim.

In shooting the ball, extend or straighten the arm toward the target, extend or flip the wrist forward and let the ball roll off the finger tips. When this technique is properly executed, the ball will have backspin rotation.

A good drill procedure in practice is to start with the hand under the ball, rotate so the wrist is cocked and the arm bent at a 90 degree angle, then extend toward the target, using only the forefinger to guide the ball toward the basket. This teaches ball control and gives the ball the right arc. The one-finger shot should not be taken during a game.

Simply consider shooting as a mechanical lever with all of the angles — shoulder, elbow, wrist and ball — lined up toward the target.

1.   FOR DRILL PURPOSES, START WITH HAND UNDER BALL.
2.   ROTATE BALL.
3.   WRIST COCKED WITH HAND SLIGHTLY
       UNDER AND BEHIND BALL.

4-5.   EXTEND ARM TOWARD TARGET.
6   FLIP WRIST FORWARD.

1-3.   CLOSE-UP OF ONE-FINGER DRILL.
        SHOULDER, UPPER ARM, ELBOW, FOREARM
        AND WRIST IN PROPER ALIGNMENT.

4-6.   ON FOLLOWTHROUGH, USE OF FORE-
        FINGER IMPROVES BALL CONTROL AND
        GUARANTEES BACKSPIN WITH PROPER ROTATION.

Lay-Up Shot Techniques

The *Lay-Up* is probably the most basic shot in basketball. When shooting a Lay-Up, the head is up and the eyes are focused at a point on the backboard where the ball is to be banked into the basket.

To achieve the shooting position, shift your weight to the foot opposite the shooting hand. Explode off the extended front foot, then drive the opposite leg upward.

During the drive upward, carry the ball in both hands to a point above and in front of the head. Release the ball to the shooting hand and extend the shooting arm fully. The palm of the shooting hand should face the basket while the ball is controlled with the fingertips.

At the release, place the ball gently against the backboard and pronate the wrist inward on the follow-through.

1. HEAD UP WITH EYES ON BACKBOARD.
2. SHIFT WEIGHT TO FRONT FOOT.
3. EXPLODE OFF FRONT FOOT; DRIVE
   OTHER LEG FORWARD AND UPWARD.

4. EXTEND SHOOTING ARM FULLY AND CONTROL
   BALL WITH FINGERTIPS.
5. WITH PALM FACING BACKBOARD, RELEASE
   BALL AGAINST BACKBOARD.
6. PRONATE WRIST ON FOLLOW-THROUGH.

Crossover Lay-Up Shot

As your drive approaches the basket, execute the techniques of the
Crossover Change Dribble to bring the dribble under control as you
rotate the shoulders and square your body to the board.

Jump off the extended inside foot and bring the ball up with both
hands, extending your arms to the point of release. Pronate the wrist
and shooting hand inward upon release of the ball to the board.

1. AS DRIVE APPROACHES BASKET,
   EXECUTE CROSSOVER CHANGE DRIBBLE.
2. ROTATE SHOULDERS AND SQUARE BODY
   TO BOARD.
3. JUMP OFF EXTENDED INSIDE FOOT.
4. WITH BALL IN BOTH HANDS, EXTEND
   ARMS TO POINT OF RELEASE.
5. PRONATE WRIST AND SHOOTING HAND IN-
   WARD UPON RELEASE OF BALL TO BOARD

Inside Power Shot Techniques

The *Inside Power Shot* is executed from a **ready position,** i.e., head up, knees flexed, and eyes focused at a point on the backboard where the ball is to be banked into the basket.

Take a lead step with foot nearest the basket. As step is taken, bounce the ball in front of the body midway between the feet. Then close the stance by bringing the rear foot forward. Simultaneously drop the center of gravity for upward jump.

Explode off both feet upward and laterally to the basket. At the same time, carry the ball upward with both hands to a point above and in front of the head. Extend the body and shooting arm fully.

Release the ball to the fingertips of the shooting hand with the palm facing the backboard. Protect the shot with the free arm and complete the shot by pronating the wrist inward on follow-through.

35

1. FROM READY POSITION, TAKE LEAD STEP
   TO TARGET.
2. DROP CENTER OF GRAVITY.
3. BRING FEET TOGETHER; CONTROL BALL
   WITH BOTH HANDS.
4. EXPLODE UP AND EXTEND BODY FULLY.
5. PROTECT SHOT WITH FREE ARM.
6. RELEASE BALL AGAINST BACKBOARD.

Jump Shot Techniques

The jump shot is made from a starting position — head up, eyes on basket and weight distributed on the balls of the feet, with the foot on the side of the shooting hand extended slightly.

Before and after the jump, the ball is controlled by both hands. Place the hand opposite the shooting hand on the side and slightly behind the center of the ball. The shooting hand is placed behind the ball.

While exploding upward, carry the ball to the shooting position with both hands. The shooting arm forms a 90 degree angle, and the eyes are focused on the basket.

Make the release when the shooting arm is at full extension and at the peak of the jump. On the release, control the shot with the fingertips and follow through by flipping the wrist forward.

1. READY POSITION, FACING BASKET WITH HEAD UP, KNEES FLEXED AND WEIGHT ON BALLS OF FEET. CONTROL BALL WITH BOTH HANDS.
2. EXPLODE UP WITH EYES ON RIM.
3. SHOOTING ARM FORMS 90 DEGREE ANGLE WITH ELBOW CLOSE TO BODY.
4. EXTEND ARM FULLY ON RELEASE.

37

Turnaround Jump Shot Techniques

The *Turnaround Jump Shot* has all the basic shooting techniques of the Jump Shot.

The fundamental differences of the Turnaround Jump Shot are: The shooter's back is to the basket when receiving the ball. The feet are parallel rather than one foot slightly foward as in the jump shot. A pivot must be made to place the shooter in position to make the shot.

Once facing the basket, all jump shot techniques apply.

1. **READY POSITION**
   Back to Basket with Head Up. Flex Knees with Feet Parallel. Weight on Balls of Feet.
2. **PIVOT TO FACE BASKET.**

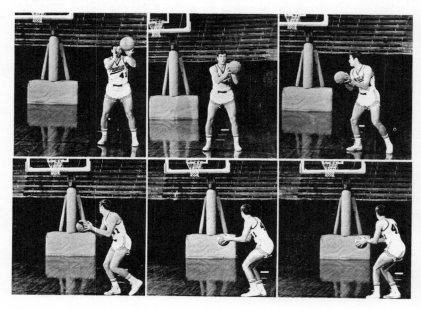

3. CONTROL BALL WITH BOTH HANDS.
4. EXPLODE UP. SHOOTING ARM FORMS
   90-DEGREE ANGLE. EYES ON RIM.
5. EXTEND ARM FULLY ON RELEASE. CONTROL
   SHOT WITH FINGERTIPS. PRONATE WRIST
   ON FOLLOW-THROUGH.

Side View (Turnaround Jump Shot)

One-Hand Set Shot Techniques

The *One-Hand Set Shot* is most commonly used at the free-throw line although it may be shot effectively around the perimeter of the keyhole.

Execute this shot from the basic offensive stance while holding the ball in front of your face, just below eye level for purposes of "sighting."

The shooting hand should be placed behind and slightly off the ball's center with the support hand placed on the side.

Initial body movement is very important in executing this shot. In one continuous motion this sequence develops: 1) knees flex slightly, 2) body (trunk) flexes at waist, 3) ball is brought down toward chin as wrist cocks, 4) ball is pushed toward basket with release coming at point of full arm extension (wrists flex) and 5) hand and wrists continue to flex on follow-through to basket.

From beginning to end, your body weight moves slightly forward to the balls of your feet. Body rhythm is all-important in executing this shot to the point of release from the fingertips.

1. FROM BASIC OFFENSIVE STANCE, HOLD BALL IN FRONT OF FACE JUST BELOW EYE LEVEL. EYES FOCUS ON RIM.
2. FLEX KNEES, BEND BODY AT WAIST.
3. BRING BALL TOWARD CHIN AS YOU COCK WRIST.
4. PUSH BALL TOWARD BASKET, MAKING RELEASE AT FULL-ARM EXTENSION. CONTROL BALL WITH FINGERTIPS.
5. PRONATE HAND AND WRIST ON RELEASE AND FOLLOW-THROUGH

Hook Shot Techniques

From a **ready position** with your back toward the basket, start your move by taking a lead step toward the takeoff point for the shot.

Rotate the body and shift your weight to the lead foot as you carry the ball upward to the point of release. Note that the ball is carried with shooting hand slightly underneath. Use the opposite hand to control the ball toward release point and protect the shot thereafter.

Jump off the lead foot (inside) and raise the opposite knee and leg upward to carry your body momentum toward the target.

The release is made as the ball is carried up in an arc toward the basket and the shooting arm extends out to the point where the ball leaves the fingertips. Your hand and wrist then rotate over the ball in line with the release on follow-through.

41

1. TAKE LEAD STEP TOWARD RELEASE
   POINT.
2. JUMP OFF INSIDE FOOT WHILE
   CARRYING BALL UPWARD WITH
   BOTH HANDS.
3. DRIVE OUTSIDE KNEE AND LEG
   UPWARD TO PROJECT BODY
   MOMENTUM TOWARD TARGET.

4. ARCH BALL TOWARD BASKET
   AND EXTEND SHOOTING ARM TO
   POINT OF RELEASE. PROTECT
   BALL WITH FREE HAND.
5. RELEASE BALL OFF FINGERTIPS
   AND ROTATE HAND OVER BALL
   IN LINE WITH RELEASE ON
   FOLLOW-THROUGH

Drive to the Basket

Receiving the Ball from a Teammate

The player who moves well without the ball and is constantly on the move most often gets free for a pass from a teammate.

Usually the most effective means of receiving a pass is to take a couple of steps toward the passer. In so doing the receiver reduces the distance and time which the defender has to intercept the ball. However, faking toward the passer or to one side, then reversing in the opposite direction, also may provide an opportunity to receive a pass safely.

1. MOVE TO GET CLEAR FOR A PASS FROM A TEAMMATE.
2. STEPPING TOWARD PASSER CUTS DOWN DISTANCE AND TIME WHICH DEFENDER HAS TO INTERCEPT BALL.
3. KEEP EYE ON BALL, MAKE CATCH AND SET UP TO MAKE A PASS, SHOT OR DRIBBLE AND DRIVE TO BASKET.

47

Drive Techniques

All drives to the basket start from the shooting or starting position. Upon moving to receive the ball from a teammate, the subsequent moves are basic to a series of possible maneuvers: the jump shot, power lay-up, long step drive and short jump shot, and step-through move for a short jump shot, the crossover long step and pull-up jump shot, and the step-through move from the crossover to a pull-up jump shot.

Go to meet the ball, pivot to face the basket and assume a starting position. Make a slight head fake upwards as if to shoot, then pull the ball across the body and with the foot opposite the fake, explode with a drive step past the defender. The ball is projected forward and to the side of the dribbling hand. Simultaneously thrust opposite or pivot foot forward to continue penetration of the drive. Protect the ball with arm and leg nearest defender.

1-2.   RECEIVING THE BALL AND FACING THE
       BASKET, GETTING INTO SHOOTING
       POSITION.

3.   IF THE LEFT FOOT IS THE PIVOT, START
       LONG STEP DRIVE TO BASKET WITH
       RIGHT FOOT.

Power Lay-Up

The power lay-up is an extension of the long step drive technique and gives the offensive player three options as he looks for a scoring play in one-on-one situations — passing to an open man, going for the lay-up or taking a jump shot after making a step-through move if stopped by a defender.

After a slight fake upwards as if to take a long jump shot, the offensive player tenses his pivot leg slightly as he prepares to push off from the ball of his foot. He then takes a driving long step in the direction he wants to go. As he gains an advantage on the defender, the ball-handler pulls up in the basket area with both feet planted solidly in an attempt to get the defensive man on his back. If he makes a power move toward the basket, the player should keep the ball in good shooting position in case he has to reset his shot to avoid a block.

Keep the body under control at all times. Do not leave your feet until taking the shot.

1. PIVOT LEG TENSES AS PLAYER PUSHES OFF,
   TAKING A DRIVING LONG STEP TOWARD BASKET.
2. AFTER GAINING ADVANTAGE ON
   DEFENDER, PULL UP IN BASKET AREA WITH
   BOTH FEET PLANTED.
3 KEEP THE BALL IN GOOD SHOOTING POSI-
   TION AT ALL TIMES.
4. DON'T LEAVE YOUR FEET UNTIL TAKING THE SHOT.

49

Long Step Drive,
Pull Up and Short Jump Shot

A forced shot rarely finds its target. Therefore, it is just as important to take a good shot near the basket as it is farther away. And it is equally important not to develop a selfish attitude in looking for a scoring play.

If, in driving toward the basket, the offensive player finds he can not continue because of the defense, he can either pull up and pass off to a teammate, or attempt a jump shot.

In taking the shot, plant the inside foot and go straight up with both feet pointed toward the basket, keeping body balance and good shooting technique in mind.

1. START LONG STEP DRIVE.
2. PULL UP AND TAKE SHORT JUMP SHOT,
    PLANTING INSIDE FOOT AND GOING UP
    WITH FEET POINTED TOWARD BASKET.

3. **KEEP BODY BALANCE AND OBSERVE GOOD SHOOTING TECHNIQUES.**

Step-Through Move

If the defense stops the basic jump shot, a quick step-through move often can be effective in getting the ball handler open for a different type of shot. If this maneuver is also blocked, he can still step back and try again for the jump shot or pass off to a teammate.

The inside foot, or the one closest to the free throw lane, is the pivot foot. In a step-through move, the outside foot is moved quickly across the defender's feet in hopes of gaining an offensive advantage by getting the defender on your back.

Then, with feet planted, re-establish body balance by squatting and moving head back. Move the ball through to the open shooting area if you can, keeping in mind fundamental shooting techniques at all times.

Keep body under control and do not leave your feet until you take the short jump shot. Otherwise, you may get caught in mid-air. As long as your pivot foot is still anchored, you can always step back if the short jump shot isn't available.

1. WHEN DEFENSE STOPS JUMP SHOT, STEP-THROUGH COULD BE NEXT MOVE.
2. WITH PIVOT FOOT PLANTED, STEP ACROSS DEFENDER WITH OUTSIDE FOOT.
3. SQUAT AND MOVE HEAD BACK TO REGAIN BALANCE.
4. DO NOT LEAVE YOUR FEET AGAIN UNLESS YOU TAKE SHORT JUMP SHOT.

Crossover Long Step
To Pull-Up Jump Shot

Go to meet ball, pivot and face basket in shooting position. Pull ball
across body and make crossover long step with drive foot and explode
past defender. As ball is thrust forward and to the side of dribbling
hand, drive opposite foot forward to continue penetration. Protect ball
against defender with arm and leg. Pull up, planting the outside foot
to re-establish balance and keeping both feet pointed toward basket.
Come straight up for jump shot, using basic shooting fundamentals
with shoulder, elbow, and hand lined up.

1. START FROM SHOOTING POSITION.
2. MAKE CROSSOVER LONG STEP DRIVE PAST DEFENDER.
3. KEEP ARM AND LEG BETWEEN BALL AND DEFENDER.
4. PULL UP, GET BALANCE, AND GO UP FOR SHOT.

Step-Through Move
After Crossover to Pull-Up Jump Shot

From a different camera angle and floor position, this shows step-through maneuver against defender when player pulls up but can't make jump shot attempt.

Offensive player steps through in attempting to gain advantage by having defender on his back. From step-through, player with ball can either shoot short jump shot or step back and attempt longer jumper or pass off to teammate.

1. MAKE STEP-THROUGH MOVE.
2. SHOULDER, ARM AND LEG PROTECT BALL FROM DEFENDER.

3. TAKE SHORT JUMP SHOT.

Crossover Drive Techniques

Go to meet ball, pivot to face basket and assume a **ready position**.

Fake in opposite direction of the intended drive, pull ball across body and, using a crossover step with foot on the side of the fake, explode past the defender.

As the ball is projected forward and to the side of the dribbling hand, drive opposite foot forward to continue penetration of the drive. Protect the ball with arm and leg nearest the defender.

1. **FAKE IN DIRECTION OPPOSITE INTENDED DRIVE.**
2. **SHIFT WEIGHT TO OPPOSITE FOOT, PULL BALL ACROSS BODY AND BEGIN CROSSOVER STEP.**
3. **CROSS OVER WITH LEAD FOOT.**
4. **DRIVE TRAILING FOOT FORWARD. CONTINUE PENETRATION. PROTECT BALL WITH ARM AND LEG.**

Rebounding

Blocking Out for Rebounds

Certainly one of the most important fundamentals in the game of basketball is blocking out for rebounds. The *block-out* is executed as soon as the offensive player can diagnose and intercept the offensive player's route to the basket.

The actual block-out is the result of the defensive man's executing either a **front pivot** or a **reverse pivot** which in effect blocks the opponent's path to the rebound.

Use the pivot which suits the situation best and the one which you can confidently and properly execute.

As soon as a shot attempt is detected, determine immediately what path the offensive player will take toward the basket. Pivot to intercept his move and into a ready position for the rebound. The pivot affords you an advantageous inside position for the rebound.

1. IMMEDIATELY AFTER SHOT IS ATTEMPTED, DETERMINE WHAT PATH "YOUR MAN" WILL TAKE TOWARD THE BASKET.
2. USE PIVOT WHICH SUITS THE SITUATION AND YOU BEST
3. PIVOT INSIDE, TOWARD THE OFFENSIVE PLAYER ON THE FRONT PIVOT.

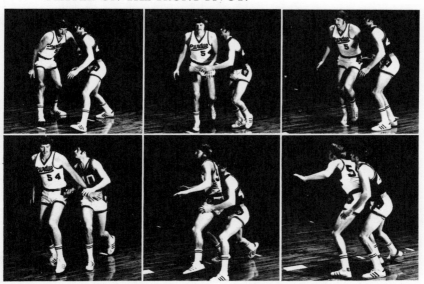

4. OR, PIVOT OUTSIDE, SLIGHTLY AWAY FROM
    THE OFFENSIVE PLAYER FOR REVERSE PIVOT.
5. SET UP IN READY POSITION FOR REBOUND.

Rebounding Techniques

With the body in a **ready position,** i.e., head up, knees flexed, eyes
on backboard, arms above the waist and feet parallel, drop center of
gravity and explode upward to full extension.

In rebounding the ball use a firm grip with fingers spread. Pull the
ball to chest level with elbows out. Upon landing, the feet should be
at least a shoulder's-width apart with knees flexed.

1. READY POSITON
    Head Up. Eyes on Ball. Arm above Waist. Knees
    Flexed. Feet Parallel. Weight on Balls of Feet.

2. **DROP CENTER OF GRAVITY AND EXPLODE UP, EXTENDING ARMS.**
3. **EXTEND BODY FULLY, GRIP BALL WITH FINGERS SPREAD.**
4. **PULL BALL TO CHEST.**
5. **FLEX KNEES ON LANDING WITH FEET A SHOULDER'S-WIDTH APART.**

Outlet Pass

From the landing position quickly pivot for an outlet pass. A Chest, Overhead or Baseball Pass is most often thrown. With a teammate nearby, a quick Flip Pass may be effective.

A quick and accurate *outlet* pass is important to get the ball down floor to set up the offense before the opponents can recover.

6. **PIVOT OUTSIDE FOR OUTLET PASS.**

Rules Simplified

Basketball Court Diagram

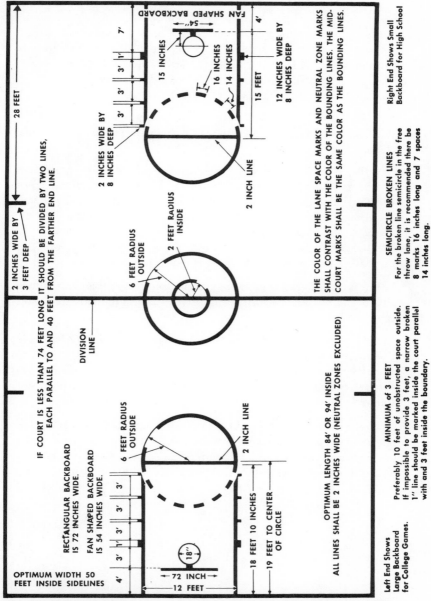

Provided through the courtesy of the National Federation of State High School Athletic Associations. *(Diagram 1)*

The Playing Area

Basketball may be played indoors or out-of-doors, although in America the game is generally played indoors. Basketball is played on a court ranging in size from a maximum of 94 feet long by 50 feet wide to a minimum of 74 feet long by 42 feet wide. Ideal measurements are:

COLLEGE AGE   94 by 50 feet
HIGH SCHOOL AGE   84 by 50 feet

The court is to have a hard surface usually of wood. There should be at least three feet (preferably ten feet) of unobstructed space on all sides of the court.

At either end of the court are backboards made of wood, glass, steel or other rigid, flat materials. The backboards must be one of two types: a rectangular board six feet long and four feet high, or a fan-shaped board. The front face of the backboard is to be four feet from the end boundary line, and parallel. The basket is attached to the center of the backboard so that the rim of the basket is ten feet from the floor. From the basket ring is suspended a white cord net.

In the exact center of the court is a circle, four feet in diameter, known as the *center circle*. A "restraining circle," 12 feet in diameter, is concentric outside the center circle.

In the center at each end of the court is a *free-throw lane*, 12 feet wide, ending in circles 12 feet in diameter. The centers of these circles are to be 19 feet from the end boundary lines. A *free-throw line* is drawn through the circle, parallel with the end boundary line. The free throw line is 15 feet from the plane of the face of the backboard.

A *division line* divides the court into two equal parts. A team's *front court* is that part of the court containing the team's own basket, that is, the basket through which a team tries to score its points. The other half of the court is known as that team's *backcourt*. For the opposing team, the names are reversed.

The Ball

A basketball is to be round, no larger than 30 inches in circumference and no smaller than 29 inches. Its weight should be no more than 22 ounces nor less than 20 ounces. When inflated, it should bounce to a height (measured to top of ball) of not less than 49 inches nor more than 54 inches after it has been dropped from a height of six feet (measured to bottom of ball). The home team is to provide the game ball.

The Team

A basketball team consists of five players, generally known as a *center*, two *forwards* and two *guards*. A team cannot begin a game with less than five players, but if it has no substitutes to replace disqualified players, it must finish the game with less than five players. A player must leave the game after committing five personal fouls, and cannot return during that game. Each player must wear a numbered shirt.

The Officials

The officials should be a referee and an umpire, assisted by two timers and two scorers. A single timer and a single scorer may be used if acceptable to both teams. Officials must conduct the game according to the rules. A third floor official is optional in many leagues.

Scorers record personal and technical fouls, and notify the referee when the fifth personal foul is called on a player. They also record time-outs charged against each team. In scoring, most scorers use the following symbols:

P1, P2, P3, etc. for personal fouls

T for technical fouls;

O for free throw attempt, X inside O if try is good;

2 for field goals.

Generally, a field goal counts two points. In some leagues, however, a field goal can count three points if it is shot from outside a designated area, usually either 19 or 22 feet from the basket. A successful free throw counts one point.

Game Times

College teams play two 20-minute halves, with a 15-minute intermission between the halves.

Teams of high school age play four eight-minute quarters, with two one-minute intermissions between the quarters and a ten-minute intermission between the halves.

Overtime Periods

If the score is tied at the end of the second half in college games, play shall continue for an extra period of five minutes, or for as many extra five-minute periods as are needed to break the tie. A one-minute intermission is taken before each extra period. The ball is put in play in the center circle at the start of each extra period.

High school games which end in ties are played off in extra periods of three minutes each, with a two-minute intermission before each extra period. A team wins when it is ahead by one point or more at the end of any extra period. The first team to lead by two points during the second extra period wins the game.

Time-outs

Each team is allowed five charged time-outs during regular play. A charged time-out is either a time-out requested by a player when the ball is dead or that player's team has control of the ball; or a time-out for an injury or removal of a disqualified player. A time-out is not charged if an injured or disqualified player is replaced with 1½ minutes. If the officials halt a game to permit a player to tie a shoelace, a time-out is not charged. Each team gets an additional time-out in each overtime period.

Some Other Rules

Visiting teams have the choice of baskets for the first half. Teams change baskets for the second half.

The score of a forfeited game is 2 to 0.

When a team gains control of the basketball in its backcourt, it must move the ball into its front court within ten seconds, unless the ball is touched by an opponent. When the ball is touched, a new play starts, and a new ten-second period is allowed.

Common Offensive Alignments

In developing team play many factors must be taken into consideration before settling upon any one offensive alignment. The alignment used is merely a vehicle whereby the team may execute certain movements which best utilize the individual talents of the team and express the philosophy of the coach. In certain strategic situations the offensive alignment is a countermove to specific defenses.

Most common offensive alignments utilize a single post situation, that is, with one pivotman playing close to the basket or no further away from the hoop than the foul line.

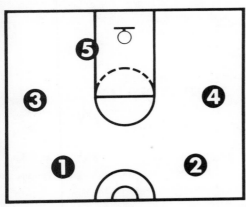

SINGLE LOW POST OFFENSIVE SETUP.
This alignment is sometimes referred to as a 2-3 *offense*. 1 and 2 are guards, 3 and 4 forwards and 5 is the center or pivotman. *(Diagram 2)*

Key to diagrams at end of Glossary

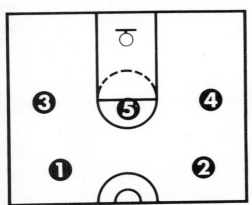

SINGLE HIGH POST OFFENSIVE SETUP.
This alignment is sometimes referred to as a 2-1-2 *offense*. The positions correspond to those of Diagram 3. *(Diagram 3)*

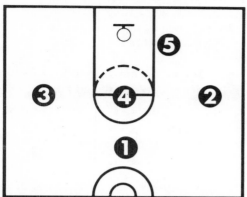

TANDEM OR 1-3-1 OFFENSIVE SETUP.
In this alignment positions are referred to by different terms. **1** is the point, **2** and **3** are wings, **4** is the *high post* and **5** is the *low post*. This setup is very popular vs certain zone defenses.
(Diagram 4)

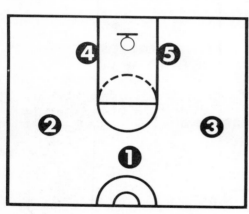

DOUBLE POST OFFENSIVE SETUP.
Sometimes referred to as a *3-2 alignment*. Players **1**, **2**, and **3** are perimeter or a combination of guards and quick forwards. **4** and **5** are low post players.
(Diagram 5)

Comparing the positions within the various offensive alignments, two important factors must be observed when considering placement of personnel: 1) the distance from the basket, and 2) whether the position requires facing the basket or back to basket.

Certain characteristics and skills are required for proficiency at each position. There is some obvious overlapping within the various types of alignments.

Guards (Small Perimeter Players)

Guards are usually the smaller of the three positions: however, size is a definite advantage if the other necessary attributes are present. Speed, quickness and agility are the most important of the physical qualities for this position. Necessary skills are: ball handling (dribbling and passing,) playmaking and outside shooting. Personnel at this position are also referred to as "floor generals" or "quarterbacks" because of their importance as team leaders on the floor. In the 1-3-1 setup they are pointmen. (Diagram 4)

Forwards (Large Perimeter Players)

Forwards or cornermen, sometimes a wing as in the 1-3-1, must possess many of the same qualities as the small perimeter players, but size is much more important because of their added responsibility as rebounders. Physical attributes necessary are height, strength, quickness and agility. Necessary skills include rebounding, passing and receiving, outside and corner shooting and ball handling for driving.

Pivotmen (High or Low Post)

Centers or pivotmen occupy the post positions which require back-to-the-basket offensive skills.

Necessary skills include inside shooting around the basket, rebounding and passing. Obviously, most important of the physical requirements are height, strength, ability to jump and mobility in traffic.

Basic Individual Offensive Maneuvers

Certain individual basketball skills are just as necessary as the aforementioned physical attributes and simple skills or fundamentals.

Recommended for all face-to-the-basket ball players is mastery of at least two or three of the following offensive maneuvers.

1. FAKE RIGHT THEN DRIVE LEFT.
   FAKE LEFT THEN DRIVE RIGHT.

2. FAKE RIGHT, LEFT THEN DRIVE RIGHT.
   FAKE LEFT, RIGHT THEN DRIVE LEFT.

3. FAKE RIGHT (HESITATE) THEN DRIVE RIGHT.
   FAKE LEFT (HESITATE) THEN DRIVE LEFT.

4. ROCKER STEP FAKE AND DRIVE RIGHT.
   ROCKER STEP FAKE AND DRIVE LEFT.

5. FAKE SHOT AND DRIVE RIGHT.
   FAKE SHOT AND DRIVE LEFT.

6. FAKE SHOT, BACK TO READY POSITION
   THEN SHOOT.

All postmen should develop at least two or three of the following back-to-the-basket maneuvers:

1. FAKE RIGHT, COME BACK LEFT AND SHOOT.
   FAKE LEFT, COME BACK RIGHT AND SHOOT.

2. FAKE RIGHT, HOOK BACK WITH LEFT FOOT
   AND SHOOT.
   FAKE LEFT, HOOK BACK WITH RIGHT FOOT
   AND SHOOT.

3. FAKE RIGHT, PAUSE THEN GO RIGHT.
   FAKE LEFT, PAUSE THEN GO LEFT.

4. FAKE RIGHT, COME BACK TO RIGHT WITH
   LEFT FOOT (FORWARD PIVOT). USE CROSS-
   OVER STEP AND SHOOT.
   FAKE LEFT, COME BACK TO RIGHT WITH
   LEFT FOOT (FORWARD PIVOT). USE CROSS-
   OVER STEP AND SHOOT.

5. **REVERSE PIVOT, FAKE RIGHT AND GO LEFT.**
   REVERSE PIVOT, FAKE LEFT AND GO RIGHT.

Basic Two- and Three-Man Offensive Maneuvers

For the most part, the game of basketball is developed around individual skills of the team; however, for the sake of teamwork and organization, team offenses are structured around a few basic two- or three-man "games" or movements. The following maneuvers are designed to set up quick scoring opportunities and stay within the framework of team play.

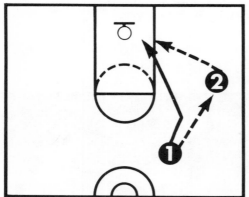

Key to diagrams at end of Glossary

GIVE AND GO MANEUVER.

1 passes to 2, sets up his defensive man wtih one or two steps toward 2 (as if to go and receive return handoff) then sharply breaks for the basket. 2 anticipates the move and makes a good lead pass to 1. *(Diagram 6)*

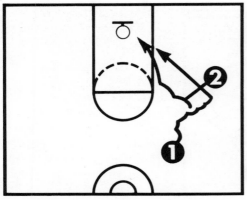

PICK AND ROLL MANEUVER.

1 dribbles at **2**'s inside shoulder forcing his defender to go behind the pick by **2**. As **1** dribbles off **2**, **2** pivots on inside foot screening off the defender to chase **1** and force a defensive switch, **1** passes to **2** who then releases for the basket. *(Diagram 7)*

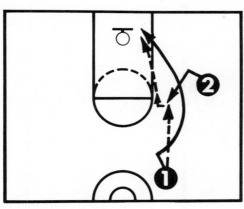

GUARD AROUND MANEUVER.

1 passes to **2**, makes a good jab-step fake, then breaks around **2** (brushing off defender). **2** pivots on inside foot and makes overhead pass to **1** cutting to basket. *(Diagram 8)*

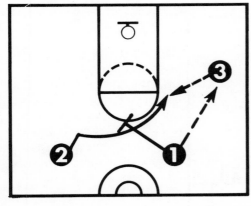

SCREEN AWAY MANEUVER

1 passes to **3** and moves away from pass to set a screen on **2**'s defender. **2** must time his cutoff, **1** allowing him to get into proper screen position, then, setting his man up, break off **1**'s block to receive pass from **3**.
(Diagram 9)

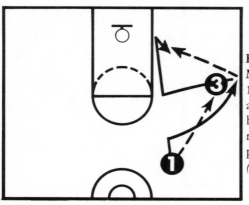

HANDOFF W/RELEASE MANEUVER.
1 passes to 3, sets his man up with a fake away from the ball then goes behind 3 to receive handback. 3 releases away and sets up in a low post position. 1 then passes to 3. *(Diagram* 10)

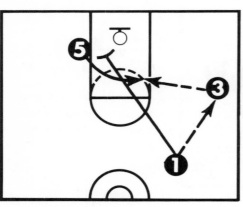

LOW POST SCREEN MANEUVER.
Using the same idea as indicated in Diagram 9 the screen away can be set to free the low post by 1 blocking 5's defender. 3 makes pass to 5 as he breaks open around screen. *(Diagram* 11)

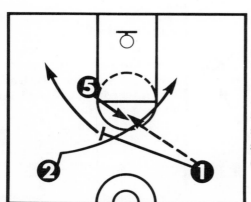

GUARD-GUARD SPLIT OFF POST MANEUVER.
1 passes to 5 in high post. 1 goes immediately to set an inside brush screen on 2's defensive man. 2's cut and 1's release occur at the same instant, creating the split action off 5. *(Diagram* 12)

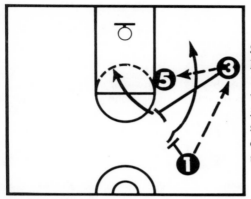

SIDE SPLIT OFF POST MANEUVER.
1 passes to 3 and sets up his man while 3 makes pass into post to 5. 3 comes and sets an inside brush screen for 1. 1's cut and 3's release occur at the same instant, creating the split action off 5. *(Diagram 13)*

Defense—Types, Theories and Skills of Play

Team defense is divided into two basic types, **man-to-man** and **zone**. A third type being used more and more today is a combination of man-to-man and zone, but it is used for special situations almost exclusively.

Coaching philosophies will vary to some degree. Basically, however, the man-to-man defense is oriented primarily toward individual player for player assignments, sometimes referred to as match-ups. Zone defenses are more oriented to ball and area of the court. Both defenses rely upon weakside (away from the ball) basket coverage based upon direction of ball movement.

In the various zone defensive alignments, players are assigned specific areas to defend whenever the ball enters their area. In the **combination defense,** usually one player will be assigned in a one-on-one man match-up while the remaining four will form a four-man zone (box or diamond). Sometimes if there is a need to defend two players on a man-to-man basis, the remaining three men will form a triangle zone.

It is most common for both basic types of defenses (man and zone) to be played with varying degrees of pressure as well as extending coverages from normal halfcourt to mid-court, three-quarter, or full-court presses. As with the selection of offensive alignments and styles of play, the same basic factors influence the selection of team defense or defenses to be employed. The quality of individual talent and coaching philosophy are weighed very heavily in determining the approach to team defense.

All factors being equal, most coaches feel that the man-to-man defense played as intended gives the best total coverage to the problems posed by the opponent's offensive strengths. Philosophies may vary for various reasons as already pointed out and for that reason as well as certain game strategies which may apply, either defense may be played very aggressively or, in varying degrees, very passively.

Basic to proper individual execution of either defense is the mastering of the fundamentals required. It is most important to develop proper defensive position with the body in a semi-crouch position with knees flexed, back straight, head up and with arms and hands comfortably spread. The feet are probably the single most important aspect of good defensive play. They must be kept spread approximately a shoulder's-width apart with a slightly staggered stance and weight primarily over the balls of the feet. The player must guard against crossing the feet with any movement and should concentrate on short, quick shifts of foot position to maintain good position defensively.

Guarding a man without the ball is a very important aspect of man defense. Anticipation of his movements, avoiding picks or screens and **preventing him from receiving the ball,** all will take hours of drilling to perfect. Communication is a must between players. All sound defensive players are alert and ready to help by talking to their teammates. With only a few exceptions the basic rule for man-to-man defense is to stay between your man and the basket, control his attempt to drive and not let him have a good percentage shot.

Like offensive alignments, there are many variations of zone defenses. Most common are: 2-1-2, 2-3, 1-3-1, 1-2-2 and the 3-2. Additionally, there are several half-court and full-court zone presses. Size, quickness and jumping (rebounding) ability are the prime factors in selecting the placement of personnel for defensive assignments within each zone defense. Usually these defensive position assignments closely parallel the same offensive positions. In some cases, coaches may make strategic changes or ''adjustments.''

In Diagram **14** the basic 2-3 zone positions are shown. The subsequent diagrams show each man's adjustment (rules of coverage) with the movement of the ball around the perimeter and into the corner.

2-3 ZONE DEFENSE COVERAGE.
Shown when the ball is out front at a normal guard position. If the offense does not provide a normal match-up for the defense, then players start to cheat in the anticipated direction of ball movement. *(Diagram 14)*

Key to diagrams at end of Glossary

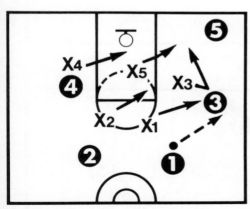

CONTINUING THE 2-3 COVERAGE.
As the ball is passed from 1 to 3, X*1* goes to cover 3, X*3* will temporarily hold until X*1* can get there, then release back. X*5* plays in line with the ball and the hoop. X*2* plays in line with the ball and the midpoint of the foul line, X*4* plays in line with the ball and the corner opposite the ball. *(Diagram 15)*

CONTINUING THE 2-3 COVERAGE.

. . . as 3 passes to 5 in the corner, X3 covers 5, X1 drops off 3 back toward basket two or three steps to prevent pass from 5 to 4. X2 plays in line with ball and midpoint of foul line. X5 plays in line with ball and the hoop. X4 plays in line with the ball and the corner opposite ball.
(Diagram 16)

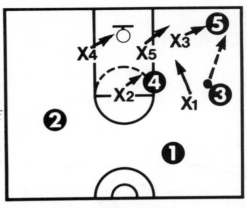

Illustrating the two popular combination zone defenses, Diagram **17** shows the box-and-one with the man-to-man "Chaser" X1 on 3.

BOX-AND-ONE DEFENSE.

In this alignment defender X1 simply tries to guard 3 as closely as possible. X2, X3, X4 and X5 play a box zone. *(Diagram 17)*

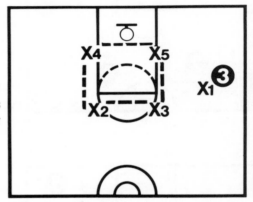

Diagram **18** shows the same situation as in Diagram **17**, except the four remaining players align in a diamond zone defense.

DIAMOND-AND-ONE DEFENSE.

The theory of defense in the diamond is identical to that of the box. Individual responsibilities are the same; however, the shifts for the box differ slightly from the diamond. *(Diagram 18)*

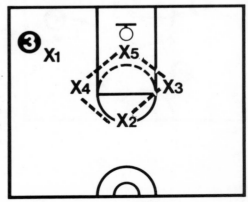

To be effective, zone defenses must function as a precision unit with all five men reacting to their assigned areas of coverage simultaneously. Good players within zone defenses know their assignment and react instinctively. Again, as in the man-to-man defense, it is most important for players to communicate at all times and always maintain good defensive positions for quick movement or shifts in position.

Editor's Note About Behind the Back Dribbles, Between the Legs Dribbles, Behind the Back Passes, etc.

Techniques presented in this book are those felt by the consultants to be fundamental to the success of any basketball team regardless of age. In recent years, more teams have begun to use such skills as the *Behind the Back Pass* and *Cross-Behind Dribble Change* which have become more widespread.

While the consultants necessarily do not discourage the use of these techniques, they do point out that such tactics need be suited to the age and skills of the team members involved. While some players become very proficient in employing such techniques, other run into considerable difficulty when attempting to do so.

Therefore, such techniques have not been described in this book since they are not considered basic to successful play.

Ball-Handling Drills

Obviously, ball handling is one of the most basic of all basketball fundamentals. The following drills are designed to develop an individual's skill in this area. Specifically, eye-hand co-ordination, hand and finger strength, and speed and rhythm with the hands are direct values derived from regular practice through these drills. Naturally, as a player develops himself in these skill aspects, he also gains self-confidence, so necessary to successful athletic competition.

The following exercises constitute a normal practice routine:

As a preface to all drills, start by slapping the ball into the receiving hand rather than merely placing it there. This will develop hand and finger strength.

The starting position for the body is shown at the left. Player should assume a semi-crouched position with the ball in front of his body at knee level. For the first two exercises the feet should be spread a shoulder's-width.
Exercise *1*

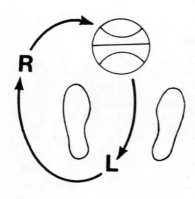

Single Leg Circle
In this exercise the player circles one leg at a time with the ball. Both legs should be circled for the complete drill. Start with the ball in the right hand in front of the body, pass the ball and bring it around the left leg to front position and into right hand. Continue this movement around one leg, then stop and start around the other leg, starting the movement with the left hand passing the ball back between the legs and circling the right leg.
Exercise *2*

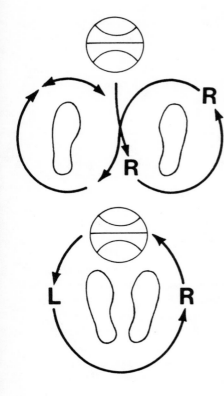

Figure "8"

Starting as in the previous exercise, keep the ball in the left hand and put it between the legs to where the right hand can receive it. The right hand then passes the ball around the right leg and back through between the legs to the left hand. Always be sure to start the ball from in front, through the legs. Exercise *3*

Around Both Legs and Body

Assume a slightly greater crouched position than in the first two exercises. Bring feet closer together and in this crouched position, carry the ball around the left side with the left hand to the right hand and then around to the front again. Change directions whenever you wish. Start with a ball around the ankles, then move it up around the knees, then straighten the body to an erect position and pass the ball around the waist. Bend over and lower the ball back down around the knees and then the ankles and back up and so on. Exercise *4*

Speed Drill (Figure "8" with Drop)

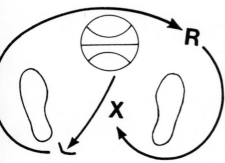

Use the same body position as in Exercises **1** and **2**. Start this exercise as a regular Figure "8" but, when bringing the ball around the left leg with the left hand, do not put the ball between the legs, but swing it on around in front and to the right which then carries the ball around the right leg and through the legs from the back side. Bring the ball to the left hand, then merely drop

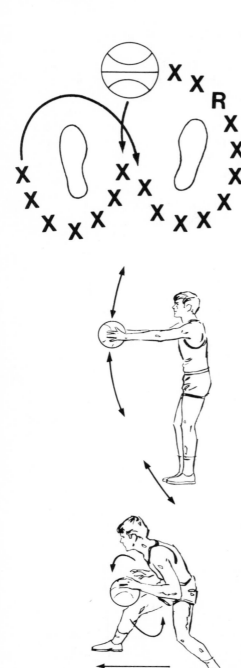

the ball to the court and quickly exchange hand positions by bringing the right arm around in front and putting the left arm to the rear. Grasp the ball with both hands as it bounces up and continue the maneuver. Exercise 5

Figure "8" Dribble (Stationary)
Use the same positions as for Exercise **2**, only this time dribble the ball with the Figure "8" pathway. Keep the ball low on the dribble. Feet may assume a slightly wide base and body may lean in the direction of the dribble. Exercise 6

Fingertips Up and Down the Body
Keep elbows stiff. Start with the ball out in front of the body at arm's length while standing erect. Tap the ball from one hand to the other as you move it above the head and down to the knees in a gradual movement. Keep your elbows stiff. When controlling the ball over the head, shuffle the feet from side to side. The "shuffle" shifts body weight from leg to leg without crossing the feet. Exercise 7

Crab Run — Putting Ball Through Legs
Assume a crouched-running position and start with an exaggerated long stride run. As you step out with the right leg, place the ball under that thigh with a left-hand to right-hand movement. Then, as the left leg comes up and forward, use a right-hand to left-hand movement to pass the ball under the left thigh.

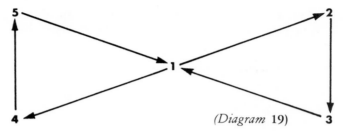

(Diagram 19)

From point 1, start your movement with a defensive slide (keeping your face forward) toward number 2. Once you reach point 2, immediately react forward, coming up on a defender with the ball to point 3, then react back in a defensive slide back to point 1. Continue this maneuver moving to point 4, back to point 5 then up to point 1 again. This should be repeated a series of five or six times without stopping. Work for quickness, keeping the body in proper defensive position throughout the drill.

Basic Passing

- Work in a one-on-one situation and learn to execute the basic passes to start a play to the corner man specifically. From a basketball position, make your fake with the ball and extend out to throw a hook pass by the opponent's ear in a quick-flip maneuver. You can change this drill by faking the flip pass high and coming around with a quick bounce pass to a teammate. It is important that you set up quick movement of the ball by faking to create an opening close to the defender between his ear and shoulder or close to his lower body for the bounce past.

Passing the Ball Against Wall

- Select a point on a wall and stand approximately three feet from it. In this maneuver, you pass the ball rapidly against the wall to receive it and pass it again immediately to the wall. This develops good quick hands and rhythm for eye-hand co-ordination.

Dribble Drill-Crossover Dribble

- On a full-length court with the basketball below waist level, take off in a zigzag manner. While dribbling to the right, cross over with a short sharp bounce in front of the body to pick up the dribble with the opposite hand in a continuous motion. Repeat this back and forth across the body for the full length of the court. it is important that you work quickly and control the ball accurately as you move down the court at full speed. It is very important to work at dribbling the ball by keeping the head and eyes up so as to build your confidence and co-ordination in dribbling without looking at the ball.

Dribble Control

- In a small six- or eight-foot area (possibly in a center jump area) have a teammate guard you closely and try to take the ball away. Keep dribbling by spinning and protecting the ball with your back and your body toward your defender. Work hard to keep the ball low and protect it by turning at every attempt the opponent makes to steal or deflect the ball.

Rope Skipping

- Spend time with the rope to develop good rhythm and body co-ordination while using rope-skipping techniques.

Change of Direction-Zigzag Drill

- In basketball it is very important for guards especially to change direction quickly while running. Start by running in a zigzag manner, then change direction sharply by pushing off the outside foot every four or five steps. Do this for the full length of the court and back. Repeat this maneuver several times each day.

Short Sprint Running

- To help develop bursts of speed which are so necessary for all basketball players, start running either on a basketball court or a smooth grasy area. Jog in a straight line with periodic ten-yard bursts of speed (sprints). Then jog a short distance. Repeat this several times each day.

One-on-One Defense

- Half-court one-on-one games are excellent competition and provide good work. They should be utilized as much as possible, putting to use the various maneuvers already described.

- A full-court one-on-one game is a tremendous conditioner. Obviously, this game will be of shorter duration than half-court one-on-one games, but much good can be derived out of working hard in a full-court situation, particularly on defensive work versus ball handling skills.

Glossary of
Basketball Terms

ASSIST: A pass to a teammate who scores directly or doesn't dribble more than twice before scoring.

BACKDOOR: An offensive maneuver in which a player cuts behind the defensive man and to the basket.

BALL CONTROL: Offensive strategy which prolongs possession of the ball by not shooting until the best possible situation develops. Also referred to as DELIBERATE OFFENSE, DISCIPLINED OFFENSE, STALL BALL, LETTING THE AIR OUT OF THE BALL.

BALL HANDLER: Player who usually brings the ball from his team's backcourt to the front court and initiates the attack. Also referred to as the PLAYMAKER.

BALL HAWK: Player who specializes in recovering loose balls.

BASE LINE: The end boundary line.

BASKET: An 18-inch ring which has a net attached to it. The object of the game is to put the ball through the basket. A team's "own" basket is the one into which team players try to throw the ball. The visiting team has the choice of baskets for the first half and the teams exchange baskets for the second half.

BENCH WARMER: A substitute.

BLOCKING: Personal contact which impedes the progress of an opponent who does not have the ball.

BOARDS: The backboards.

BONUS FREE THROW: A second free throw awarded to a shooter who is successful on his first attempt. This bonus is in effect for each common foul (except a player control foul) committed by a player whose team has committed six or more personal fouls in a half (or four or more in a half of a game played in quarters).

CHARITY STRIPE: The free-throw line, thus, the term CHARITY SHOT.

CONTROL: A player is in control when he is holding or dribbling a live ball. Team control exists when a live ball is being passed between members of a team.

CONVERSION: A successful free throw.

CRIPPLE: An easy, unopposed shot at the basket. Also called a CRIB, CRIP SHOT or SNOWBIRD.

DISQUALIFIED PLAYER: A player who is removed from further participation in a game because he has committed his fifth personal foul, or for some other reason such as a flagrant foul.

DOUBLE DRIBBLE: A violation which occurs when a player continues dribbling after grasping the ball with both hands.

DUNKING: Reaching above the rim to put the ball through the basket. Also called a STUFF SHOT. Now a violation in NCAA and high school basketball.

FAST BREAK: Offensive strategy in which a team attempts to bring the ball into scoring position before the defense can set up. Also referred to as RUN AND GUN, RUN AND SHOOT or FIREHOUSE BASKETBALL.

FOUL: A rules infraction for which the penalty is one or more free throws (except in the case of a double foul or a player control foul.) Fouls consist of the following types:

    (a)   **Common Foul:** A personal foul that is neither flagrant nor intentional nor committed against a player trying for field goal nor part of a double or multiple foul.

    (b)   **Double Foul:** Opponents commit simultaneous personal fouls against each other.

    (c)   **Flagrant Foul:** A violent or savage unsportsmanlike act or a non-contact vulgar or abusive display; not necessarily intentional.

    (d)   **Intentional Foul:** One which the official judges to be designed or premeditated; not based on severity of the act.

    (e)   **Multiple Foul:** Two or more teammates commit simultaneous personal fouls against the same opponent (a "gang-up").

    (f)   **Personal Foul:** Involves contact with an opponent while the ball is alive or after the ball is in possession for a throw-in.

    (g)   **Player Control Foul:** A common foul committed by a player while he or a teammate is in control of the ball.

    (h)   **Technical Foul:** Usually a non-contact foul by either a player or a non-player; occasionally a contact foul when the ball is dead.

    (i)   **Unsportsmanlike Foul:** Unfair, unethical or dishonorable conduct.

FREE THROW: Opportunity given to a player to score one point by an unimpeded shot from behind the free-throw line.

FRONT COURT, BACKCOURT: A team's front court is in the area of the court between the mid-court line and its basket. A team's backcourt is the rest of the court including the opponent's basket.

FULL COURT PRESS: Defense strategy in which a team guards the opposition closely in the backcourt as well as the front court. This device can employ both zone and man-to-man principles.

FUMBLE: Accidental loss of control of the ball by dropping it or permitting it to slip out of one's hands.

GIVE AND GO: Offensive strategy in which a player passes to a teammate and then cuts for the basket expecting a return pass.

GOAL TENDING: Touching the ball or the basket while the ball is on, above or within the opponent's basket.

HELD BALL: Occurs when two opponents grasp the ball so firmly that control cannot be maintained without undue roughness; a closely-guarded player (defensive player is no more than six feet away) holds the ball in his front court for five seconds; a team in its front court holds the ball for five seconds in an area enclosed by screening teammates or a closely-guarded player dribbles or combines holding the ball and dribbling for five seconds within a few feet of a front court boundary intersection or in his mid-court area.

HIGH POST: An offensive pivotman who stations himself in or near the outer half of the free-throw circle.

HITCHHIKER: The member of a three-man officiating team who remains fluid near the mid-court line.

HOLDING: Personal contact with an opponent which interferes with his freedom of movement.

HOOP: The basket. Also called CAGE or the BUCKET.

JUMP BALL: A method of putting the ball in play by tossing it up between two opponents in one of the three circles.

KEY: The free-throw lane and circle. Also called KEYHOLE.

KICKING THE BALL: A violation when done as a positive act. Accidental contact is not a violation.

LOW POST: An offensive maneuver in which the center stations himself just outside the free-throw lane close to the basket.

MAN-TO-MAN DEFENSE: A defensive system in which each player guards an assigned individual.

93

OVERTIME: One or more extra periods used to break a tie score.

PASS: Movement of the ball from one player to another, usually by throwing, bouncing or rolling along the floor.

PIVOT: Movement in which a player while holding the ball steps any number of times with the same foot, while the other foot (pivot foot) holds its point of contact with the floor.

ROLL: A movement by a screener after his teammate begins a drive off the screen. This is most effective if the defenders are forced to switch and can result in a basket for the man rolling.

SCREEN: A legal method of blocking a defender without causing contact. Screens can be set for moving players as well as stationary players and the player for whom the screen is set may or may not have the ball.

THROW-IN: A method of putting the ball in play from out of bounds.

TIME LINE: The division line across mid-court, so called because the offensive team must advance the ball across it to the front court within ten seconds after gaining possession.

TURNOVER: Any loss of possession without a shot being taken.

TWO (OR THREE) ON ONE: Two (or three) players converging on the basket with only one defensive player to attempt to stop them.

ZONE DEFENSE: A defensive system in which players cover assigned court areas, rather than specific individuals.

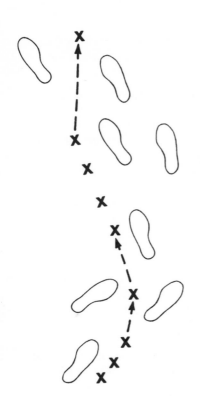

Continue on down the court as fast as you can with this drill. Ball makes the same movement as in the stationary Figure "8" Drill. Exercise *8*

Zigzag Dribble Between Legs
Begin dribbling to the right, then dribble the ball under the right leg (on the forward step) with a low sharp bounce crossing over and into the left hand. Immediately change direction of body movement to the left (as diagramed) and execute the same crossover bounce under the left leg on the third dribble in that direction.

Work for greater maneuverability and more speed as you improve. Exercise *9*

Basic Conditioning and Fundamental Drills
Tapping Against Backboard

- Tap on both sides of the backboard with left and right hand respectively 15 times each. Begin the drill by throwing the ball up to the board and tapping the ball a minimum of three times before tipping it into the basket. Keep your arm fully extended when making a tap and keep the ball controlled off the finger tips. Continuous jumping will help develop the legs and body co-ordination.

Jump Shooting

- Practice your jump shooting facing the basket by taking a quick dribble or two both to your left and to your right for the jump shot. Concentrate on making your shooting motion one continuous smooth movement. Get up to the height of your jump before releasing the

Basketball

shot. Make sure that the free hand is used to support the ball until the split-second of release of shot. Make your release at the height of your jump.

- Have a friend rebound your shot and throw it out to you. Receive the pass, maintain body control, stop and jump-shoot. It is extremely important to be able to receive a pass on the run, stop and execute a jump shot properly. Receive the pass, stop under control, jump and release your shot toward the basket. Come down, make a fake in the opposite direction with a quick jab step, turn and break hard to an area approximately 10 to 15 feet in the opposite direction to receive your next pass. Stop and repeat the same shooting maneuver as described. Do this until you have made 15 baskets. Change the areas in which you practice often.

Foul Shooting

- Concentrate on proper mechanics and body rhythm for release of the shot. It is recommended that you step back from the free-throw line and establish a new foot position with each shot.

Defensive Footwork Maneuvers

- Assume the defensive position to get into a good, naturally comfortable stance with one foot slightly in front of the other and weight evenly distributed over both feet, primarily on the balls of the feet. Get your hands in a good defensive position and keep them fairly close to your body. From this position, start your boxer shuffle. Shuffle without crossing your feet at any time. First, make your movement to the left, then back to your right. Change direction by going forward, backward left, right, forward and backward. This is excellent for your footwork and for your body balance. Make sure your steps are short and quick in your movement.

Defensive Retreating Drill

- Start from the defensive position already described by turning in and running four or five steps. Then roll the lead foot back-across the body and make a complete pivot turn while you are running. This is good for body balance and co-ordination when running in a defensive position.

Change of Direction-Triangle Drill

- Note the five numbers below (Diagram 19) and set up this situation on a court so that approximately 5 to 6 feet are between each point (number). Assume the defensive position already described above.

Key to Diagrams

❶   Offensive player with identifying number

❶.   Offensive player with ball

X1   Defensive player with identifying number

– – – – – – ➤   Direction of a pass

———————➤   Direction of movement or a cut by a player

X X X X   Dribbling basketball

                Cut, jab step, fake with change of direction

                Screen or block